CHAMPION SPORT

BIOGRAPHIES

MUHAMMAD ALI

CHAMPION SPORT

BIOGRAPHIES

MUHAMMAD ALI

JAMES DUPLACEY

Warwick Publishing Inc.

Toronto Los Angeles

www.warwickgp.com

We acknowledge the financial support of the Government of Canada through the Book Publishing Industry Development Program for our publishing activities.

ISBN: 1-894020-50-2

Published by Warwick Publishing Inc.
162 John Street, Suite 300, Toronto, Ontario, Canada M5V 2E5
1300 North Alexandria Avenue, Los Angeles, California 90027

Distributed in the United States and Canada by Firefly Books Ltd.
3680 Victoria Park Avenue, Willowdale, Ontario M2H 3K1

Cover design: Heidi Gemmill
Layout: Kimberley Young
Editorial Services: Joseph Romain
Photos: AP/Wide World Photos

Printed and bound in Canada.

Table of Contents

Factsheet

Muhammad Ali

Born Cassius Marcellus Clay, Jr., January 17, 1942

Amateur record — 103 wins, 5 defeats

Pro record — 57 wins, 5 defeats

Gold medal, 1960 Summer Olympic Games, Rome, Italy

WBA Heavyweight title February 25, 1964, over Sonny Liston

North America Boxing Federation Heavyweight title July 26, 1971 over Jimmy Ellis

Regained NABF Heavyweight title, September 10, 1973, over Ken Norton

Regained WBF Heavyweight title, October 30, 1974, over George Foreman

Regained WBF Heavyweight title, September 15, 1978, over Leon Spinks

Announced retirement, June 27, 1979

Lost comeback fight against Larry Holmes, October 2, 1979, in 10th round TKO.

Lost final professional bout versus Trevor Berbick on December 11, 1981

Introduction

It is Saturday, September 28, 1998, and the most popular event on the Australian sporting calendar is about to start in Melbourne. It is called the "Grand Final." The North Melbourne Kangaroos will be playing against the Adelaide Crows to decide who will be the champions of the Australian Football League.

Australian football is a bit different from the football played in North America. The players do not wear helmets or pads, and there are very few breaks in the 60-minute game. It is a wild, exciting sport, and Australians love it. On Grand Final Saturday, the entire country comes to a virtual stand-still. The shops are closed, the streets are empty, and the pubs are full.

The prime minister of Australia and other important government officials sit in a private box at the stadium. On the field, a lavish pre-game show is put on by dancers, acrobats, actors, singers, and musicians. Many of them are major stars on the stages of "the Land Down Under."

Each act is greeted with warm, but mainly polite, applause. The sell-out crowd is saving its big cheers for a special moment and a special guest.

Near the end of the ceremonies, this Grand Final Guest of Honor is introduced. A convertible enters the stadium and begins a slow, snail-paced crawl around the oval-shaped playing field. In the car sits Muhammad Ali. The massive crowd of more than 80,000 people rises as one and greets the former heavyweight boxing champion of the world with an ear-shattering, 20-minute standing ovation.

Ali can barely raise a single hand to greet his audience. He suffers from a serious illness that makes it difficult for him to move. Then Ali gathers strength from his adoring fans, just as he had when he was the best boxer of his generation. He begins to playfully throw a few jabs. Although he hasn't stepped into the ring since December 11, 1981, Ali still packs a powerful punch.

Only one American athlete could upstage Australia's most-watched sporting event. That athlete is Muhammad Ali.

Ali remains the world's most famous athlete. He may even be more famous now than when he was at the height of his boxing success. He is a complex individual. It is difficult to separate the myth from the man. To understand the man, you have to understand what America was like when Muhammad Ali was growing up.

In the southern United States in the 1950s, black people could not eat in white restaurants. They could not sit at the front of a public bus. Blacks had to drink from separate water fountains and live on the outskirts of cities and towns. They were not able to attend white schools, colleges, or universities. They were not allowed to vote. It was into this separate society that Muhammad Ali was born. This is his story.

Chapter 1

Cassius Marcellus Clay, Jr.

Muhammad Ali was born in Louisville, Kentucky, on January 17, 1942, and christened Cassius Marcellus Clay, after his father. He was also named for a Clay ancestor, a remarkable white politician who worked to get rid of slavery in the United States in the 1800s. The original Cassius Clay was a speaker and politician who campaigned for Abraham Lincoln in the 1860 presidential election.

Another white ancestor, Henry Clay, served as secretary of state. He introduced legislation that started the slow process of eliminating slavery. Muhammad Ali's father was proud of his family's unique heritage.

You can imagine young Cassius's surprise when he discovered that these two great "influences" on his family were white men, not black. Cassius was confused. He was hurt. He couldn't understand how his father could be so proud of these white men. It seemed to him that all they had in common was a name. They hadn't been forced to eat in different restaurants, go to blacks-only schools, or stay on their "own side of town."

Some time later, a teacher helped him understand. She told Cassius that despite all of Henry Clay's work to abolish slavery, he still felt the white race was better than the black race. That discovery had a strong effect on the young Cassius Clay. Not only did he no longer admit he had white ancestors, he often felt ashamed of the connection. "My white blood comes from slave masters," he would say. "Black blood is purer."

Although he wasn't raised in poverty, the Clay family was far from well off. Ali's father was a sign painter with a nasty temper who was often away from home. His mother, Odessa, was a cleaning lady who never earned more than four dollars a day. Money was scarce. Odessa was often so tired from working 14 hours a day, she didn't have the energy to cook supper. Many nights, Cassius and his younger brother Rudy went to bed hungry.

There were no free rides for a black family in Louisville, and that included transportation to school. In Louisville in the 1950s, there were no school buses. If you needed to take a bus to school, you had to take a city bus. That meant paying for bus tickets. Cassius's mother rarely had enough money to buy tickets for both him and Rudy. So, as the older brother, Cassius was usually the one who had to walk.

But instead of feeling sorry for himself, Cassius made the whole thing into a game. He would run to school and try to beat the bus. And most of the time, he *did* beat that bus. Years later, he said it was this type of discipline that helped him in his boxing training.

As a young boy, Cassius had a confident, cocky swagger. And he just loved to talk. Friends remember him as a kid who needed to be in the spotlight. Now we know that he was trying to cover up the fact that he thought he was stupid. Why did he feel that way? It was because he couldn't read very well. Later in his life, he would learn that he had a form of "word blindness" called dyslexia. People with dyslexia have difficulty learning to read and write. We know now that it has nothing to do with how smart you are. But Cassius Clay didn't know that. All he knew was that he could make up poems and tell funny jokes and stuff, but he couldn't write them down.

So, sometimes his frustration got the better of him. If causing trouble was the only way to get the attention he needed, then that's the path Cassius would take. He ran with a few gangs, tossed a few rocks through a few windows, and generally raised havoc. It was nothing serious, but enough to make the local police aware of this energetic young kid.

Cassius seemed to be on a track that might lead him into more serious crimes as he got older. Two events were about to occur that would determine the path Cassius Clay would walk as an adult.

The first event was the death of a black boy Cassius never even knew. Emmett Till was murdered by a gang of white youths in Sunflower County, Mississippi. He was killed simply because of the color of his skin.

Emmett's death outraged blacks and whites alike, but it struck a particular chord with Cassius Clay. He wasn't exactly sure why he felt so bad, but he mourned Emmett's death for weeks. Cassius's mother remembers him crying for days after he heard about this innocent boy who was so brutally killed.

Later, Cassius found out that he was not only the same age as Emmett, but also had the same birthday. When he learned of this, Cassius took it as a message. He believed the message was that he had been chosen by some higher power to work for the African-American people. Cassius wasn't sure how he was going to do this, but another event was about to show him the way.

When Cassius was 12 years old, his parents used much of their savings to buy a bicycle for him and his brother. Cassius could use it to get to school instead of having to run every day. His parents also hoped it would help him find a positive outlet for his boundless energy.

One rainy afternoon, Cassius and his best pal Johnny Willis went to the Columbia Gym where the annual Louisville Home Show was being held. The Home Show was a like a giant flea market, but the boys weren't shopping — they were eating. There were loads of free cookies and popcorn at the Home Show. Since Cassius didn't always get a meal at home, he jumped at the chance to score some free food.

When Cassius and Johnny left the gym, they discovered that Cassius's bike had been stolen. Cassius was very angry — and scared. He knew his father's temper and he wasn't keen on getting his backside scorched for losing his bike. His friend Johnny persuaded Cassius to report the stolen bike to the police. That way, his parents might go a little easier on him. It was a decision that would change the history of boxing.

The cop Cassius and Rudy reported to was a white patrolman named Joe Martin. As Joe listened to the boy's story, he couldn't help but notice that Cassius was a raw bundle of energy. Joe asked Cassius what he would do to the person who stole his bike. Cassius replied that "he'd beat him up bad." Patrolman Martin then asked him if he knew how to fight. Cassius said no, but he'd fight the bike thief anyway.

Joe told the two lads he would take care of everything, including explaining the situation to Cassius's parents. But he wanted something in exchange. He told Cassius that he ran an after-school boxing program. He wanted Cassius to join up. After all, if Cassius really wanted to fight, he should learn the right way to do it. Joe knew it would get the kid off the street and go a long way towards teaching him a little discipline.

When Cassius first put on boxing gloves, Joe Martin could see that he was a natural. He had coordination, balance, and a desire to learn. Soon, Cassius was spending every spare minute at the gym. He watched and listened, soaking up all the knowledge Joe could give him.

What impressed Joe the most was Cassius's desire to learn how to use defense as a weapon. Most young fighters just want to crash and bash, but Cassius was different. He seemed to understand that the best offense was a good defense. After all, if the other guy can't get to you, how can he beat you?

This understanding of defense would become the secret to Cassius Clay's success in the ring. He became a champion because he never let his opponent hurt him. How did he do that? He developed a unique strategy. Most boxers throw a punch, then move away so they don't get hit back. Cassius wanted to save his energy. So instead of moving away, he'd lean back just far enough to avoid being hit. Nobody believed it would ever work — except Cassius.

Once he had discovered boxing, Cassius worked very hard to become the best boxer he could be. Even though at age 13 he was still going to school, working as a janitor, and training for a couple of hours with Joe Martin, Cassius still had energy and ambition to spare. So he signed up to train with Freddie Stoner, one of Louisville's best boxing teachers. Cassius would work out with Stoner from eight o'clock to midnight.

Cassius also had attitude to spare. He would tell everyone who would listen — and most of those who wouldn't — that he was going to the greatest fighter of all time. His constant boasting and badgering made the older kids mad. But when they found themselves in the ring with the young man who would soon be nick-named the "Louisville Lip," they learned Clay wasn't bragging. In the ring, Cassius let his fists do the talking. And they spoke loudly, saying, "I am the greatest."

Over the next six years, Cassius became a local celebrity. He won two National Golden Glove titles (the highest amateur award in the United States) and two National Amateur titles. In his years as an ama-teur, Cassius would win a total of 103 fights and lose only 5. You can bet the next time he stepped in the ring with the five fellows who beat him, they were given a good old-fashioned whipping.

Cassius's eyes were on the prize of becoming the world heavyweight boxing champion. Many sponsors and managers were eager to do business deals with this promising young athlete. However, his coaches encouraged him to look towards another goal first, a gold medal at the 1960 Olympic Games in Rome.

Cassius agreed to turn his focus in that direction, but he had one request. He wanted to fight as a light-heavyweight. That way, his brother Rudy would get a chance to go to the Olympics too.

Boxing is divided into different classes according to how much the boxers weigh. Only one boxer could represent each weight class on the United States Olympic team. Rudy Clay was a big boy. He weighed well over 200 pounds. That meant he could only fight as a heavyweight. If Cassius remained a heavyweight, Rudy would have to beat him to get there. It was highly unlikely that Rudy would be able to do that.

So Cassius's coaches agreed to allow Cassius to fight in the light-heavyweight class, and Cassius began to train for the ultimate achievement in any amateur boxer's career: winning Olympic gold.

Chapter 2

The Golden Boy

Cassius Clay trained hard during the summer of 1960 to get ready for the Olympic Games. He ran countless miles. He took thousands of right hands to the stomach and hundreds of left jabs to the chin. Cassius was sure he was going to win a gold medal in Rome.

Unfortunately, his brother Rudy didn't make the team. Cassius would be going to the Olympics on his own. But he was confident he would find some new friends along the way.

Once he arrived in Italy, it seemed like the whole country was Cassius Clay's friend. No one in Italy saw him as a "black" boxer. They saw him as a young man with spirit, humor, and talent. He was an instant hit among the athletes in the Olympic Village where all the teams stayed. He became a front-page story in the local newspapers. He was a walking, talking hero to the kids who followed his every move. And of course, Cassius had the mouth to bring every story to life.

Once he stepped into the boxing ring, Cassius proved there was plenty of muscle behind the mouth. Olympic matches are only three rounds long. That meant that Cassius, who was in tip-top shape, could go all-out for much of the bout.

He defeated his first opponent, Yan Becaus of Belgium, in two rounds. His next victim was the 1956 middleweight gold-medal winner, Gennady Schatkov. Schatkov managed to last all three rounds, but still lost a unanimous decision to the brash Yank. Tony Madigan, an Australian pug who boasted that Clay would be putty in his hands, took a bad beating. Madigan managed to stay on his feet, but Cassius was the winner.

With those three victories, Cassius was assured of a spot in the gold-medal final match. He would be fighting against one of the world's greatest amateur boxers, three-time European champ Zbiginiew Pietrzykowski. Upon hearing his opponent's name, Cassius quipped, "I don't know how to spell it and I don't know how to say it, but once I'm through with him, no one will remember it."

The crafty Polish champion, who had 231 fights under his belt, kept the match close for the first two rounds. But Cassius moved in for the kill in the third round. When the final bell rang, all five judges named him as the clear winner.

Cassius's victory gave the USA its third consecutive light-heavyweight Olympic gold medal.

The American's win came at a time of great tension between the USA and the communist Soviet Union. At the press conference after the gold-medal final, a Soviet sportswriter tried to score some points of his own. He asked Cassius how he felt about the fact that there were still restaurants in the USA he wasn't allowed to eat in because of the color of his skin. In typical Cassius fashion, Clay shot from the lip, rhyming off a response he would later come to regret.

"Look here, Commie," he began, "we got the biggest and the prettiest cars. We got all the food we can eat. America is the greatest country in the world, and as far as places I can't eat goes, I got lots of places I can eat — more places I can than I can't."

When he returned to Louisville later in the month, Cassius was treated like a conquering hero. His home was decorated with dozens of flags. The steps were painted red, white, and blue. There were promises of parades and a big celebration at city hall.

But all that would have to wait. The first order of business was to get a sponsor and some hard-earned cash for Cassius. Now that he had achieved his goal of winning Olympic gold, it was time to turn professional.

Professional athletes usually have managers, agents, and business partners who help run their careers. In return, these people get a portion of the money the athlete earns. Cassius was a great athlete who would likely win a lot of money in his professional boxing matches. He also had a lot of charisma that made him even more popular. A number of people were hoping to represent Cassius in the professional boxing world, because they knew he was going to be very successful.

When Cassius returned from Rome, his manager at the time, Billy Reynolds, and his early mentor, Joe Martin, picked him up at the airport in New York. They took him out to fancy restaurants and showed him the sights in the Big Apple.

Billy Reynolds was from the family that owned and operated Reynolds Aluminum Products. It was one of the richest and fastest-growing companies in the USA. Reynolds wanted to handle Clay's business affairs.

But Cassius had a bad feeling about it. He had worked for the Reynolds family in the summer of 1960. Cassius felt they had treated him badly, almost like a slave. He found the Reynolds family never looked him in the eye when they talked to him. They never made him feel he was anything more than their "boy." So when Reynolds and Martin offered Cassius a business contract, he refused. There would be other offers.

Back in Louisville, Cassius and his father made plans for his future. They studied each offer carefully. The great Archie Moore, the light-heavyweight champion of the world, wanted to take Cassius under his wing. Floyd Patterson, one of America's best boxers, and his manager made Cassius an offer that was hard to ignore. But it wasn't until a lawyer representing 10 of Louisville's richest citizens approached them with a guarantee of big bucks that Cassius and his father made their decision.

This crew of millionaires headed by liquor salesman Louis Faversham became known as the "Louisville Group." They gave Cassius a large bonus for signing a contract with them, and guaranteed him much, much more in the future.

The signing was front-page news around Kentucky. It even received more than its fair share of praise in Sunday morning sermons. The message was the same in each one: Praise the Lord, a black man can make it in a white man's world. The preacher at the Ship of Zion Baptist Church put it this way: "May Cassius Clay be eternally grateful for what those kind Christian millionaires are doing for his black soul."

By now, everybody in Louisville knew who Cassius Clay was. He was difficult to ignore. Cassius never took off his Olympic gold medal, wearing it around his neck day and night. He showed it to every passing car, train, plane, and boat. He felt it was his highway to glory and there was nothing that could stop him now. *Time* magazine featured an exclusive story on him. *Life* magazine was negotiating a deal with his family. The local newspaper asked him to compose a poem about his victory in Rome, part of which went:

To make America the greatest is my goal
So I beat the Russian, and I beat the Pole
And for the USA won the Medal of Gold
Italians said, "You're greater than the Cassius of old."
(from *The Greatest: My Own Story*,
by Muhammad Ali)

Not exactly Shakespeare, but the kid did have a way with words.

Shortly after signing his new deal, Cassius and his family were honored at Louisville's city hall. The mayor made a big deal out of Clay's speech to the Soviet sportswriter about being unable to eat in some restaurants because he was black. It made Cassius pause and consider his comments. In later years, a wizened Muhammad Ali would say that he felt embarrassed when he heard his words being read back to him.

After the celebration, Cassius and Ronnie King, a close buddy, were cruising around town on their new motorcycles when they spotted a bunch of "hogs" — souped-up motorcycles — parked in front of a restaurant. Cassius and Ronnie decided to step into the "whites only" restaurant for a hamburger and a milkshake.

Cassius had never done anything like this before. Going against the "whites only" rules that existed in

Kentucky at that time could be dangerous for a black person. But now that he was the Olympic champion and a nationally known hero, Cassius was sure that the white folks would praise and honor him like his black fans. He was wrong.

Cassius and Ronnie walked into the restaurant. A silence immediately fell upon the room. A more reasonable man would have turned around and run as fast as his legs would carry him. But Cassius was hotheaded. In a corner sat a group of tough old bikers. This was not a friendly bunch of boys. If the rumors were right, this was the same crew that had beat a young black man senseless the week before.

After sitting in the restaurant for a few minutes, Cassius demanded some service. The waitress, a feeble-looking black lady, told Cassius she wasn't allowed to serve him.

Cassius stood up and said, "But I'm Cassius Clay. The champ. I'm the gold medal winner. Look." He took off his gold medal and showed it to the crowd.

Just then, the white owner came out. He made it clear that he didn't care who Clay was or what he had won — they didn't serve black people in his place. He used some very offensive language to make sure the two young men got his hateful message.

The words stung Cassius. It hurt him more than any of the punches he had absorbed in a boxing ring. Clay couldn't believe that someone in his own home town would say that. He pleaded, "But you all know me. I was born in General Hospital, only a block away. I've brought back an Olympic gold medal for my country."

The owner didn't care. To him, Cassius was just another black kid with an attitude. He nodded to the group of bikers in the corner. The mean-looking men all stood up and surrounded the two boys. It was clear they were quite capable of handing out some serious punishment.

Cassius and Ronnie slowly backed out of the restaurant and headed for the parking lot. A few of the gang members followed them and caught them just outside the eatery. One of them grabbed Cassius and tried to rip the gold medal from his neck. Cassius struggled free. He and Ronnie grabbed their bikes and took off out of there.

They tried to make it to the black neighborhood, but "Frog", the gang leader and "Kentucky", one of his deputies, caught up with Cassius and Ronnie near the Jefferson County bridge.

When your life is on the line, adrenaline takes over. Your body tells you to take action to protect yourself. Ronnie jumped off his machine, but not before aiming it right at Frog. Ronnie's bike collided with Frog's and that took care of him.

Kentucky made a run at Cassius, lassoing a huge bike chain over his head. Just as the mad biker reached him, Cassius grabbed the chain. He knocked

"Kentucky" half-way to Indiana. Ronnie then grabbed the chain and wrapped it around Frog's neck. One more tug and Frog would have been toast. The bleeding biker made a tearful plea for his life. When Ronnie released him, the two biker goons made a bee-line for safety.

Now that he and Ronnie were out of immediate danger, Cassius paused to catch his breath. At that moment he realized it made no difference what he did in his life. He could have more money than a white man. He could be more famous than a white man. But no matter how rich or well known he became, he would never have the respect of a white man.

Cassius walked to the middle of the bridge. He took the gold medal from around his neck and angrily threw it into the Ohio River.

"For the first time, I saw it for what it really was. Ordinary," Cassius would write years later. "It was just an object. My medal was gone, but ... I felt calm and relaxed. My holiday as a White Hope was over. I felt a new, secret strength."

Chapter 3

The Louisville Lip

The incident at the restaurant and later at the bridge had a strong effect on Cassius Clay. His life would never be the same. Shortly after the unscheduled bout with the motorcycle mashers, Cassius and his managers put his career on a road that would eventually lead to the peak of heavyweight boxing. It was either that or take the risk that the kid wouldn't even be alive to fight for the title.

It was decided that Cassius would start off his professional career with a warm-up bout against a local tomato can named Tunney Hunsaker. "Tomato can" is a term used to describe fighters who can take a beating but can't hurt you. Like tomato cans, these guys may dent, but they never break. They act as measuring sticks of a fighter's skills.

Cassius's fight with Tunney on October 29, 1960, showed his skills were a bit rusty. He was also a tad nervous, but he still got in some good shots. He escaped with a six-round decision in his favor.

With his professional boxing debut out of the way, it was time for Cassius to find a solid trainer. He needed someone who could get him ready to fight for the world heavyweight boxing title. The Louisville Group sent Cassius to California to train with Archie Moore, the light-heavyweight champion of the world.

Moore had held his crown since 1952, but he realized his career was coming to an end. He was now looking for a young boxer he could help train to become the best in the world.

At first, Cassius and Archie seemed to make a good team. Archie Moore was a hard nut to crack. He was a disciplinarian who wouldn't — and couldn't — accept anything but total dedication. Cassius had always prided himself on his ability to work long and hard hours.

But Archie Moore didn't just want to refine Cassius's style, he wanted to change it. Cassius had his own strong ideas about how he should be trained. The two could not agree on a training plan, and Cassius was soon looking for a new trainer.

Cassius headed back to Kentucky. When he got back home, he got a new trainer named Angelo Dundee. Dundee had worked for seven boxing champs. He was known as a good "cut-man." No one is more important to a fighter than a cut-man. When a boxer is cut during a fight, it usually looks a lot worse than it is. The trouble comes when the blood starts getting in the boxer's eyes. Then he can't see and he can get really hurt. So when a boxer is cut, the referee often has no choice but to stop the bout and give the win to the other guy. But a good cut-man can close even the deepest wound and keep his fighter in the game.

Angelo Dundee had the hands of a surgeon and the tricks of a magician. He was also known as a soft-spoken man who could offer Cassius counselling, advice, and the benefits of his many years in and out of the ring.

Dundee would serve a dual role. He would be both Cassius's manager and his trainer. Now all Cassius needed was some scrub men and some sparring partners. Scrub men rub a boxer's muscles between rounds to keep them warm. Sparring partners act as human punching bags, giving fighters the chance to practice all their moves. Soon Cassius had all these people on his team. Now he was ready to train for the big fight.

Actually, Cassius had met Angelo Dundee long before the man became his trainer. Cassius had always admired one of the boxers in Dundee's stable, a tough old slugger named Willie Pastrano. One day, Cassius walked into Dundee's gym, introduced himself, and asked if he could go a few rounds with Willie.

Dundee looked down at Cassius. With fatherly calm he told the young man that he couldn't take responsibility for the damage that Willie would do to Cassius's face. But Cassius would not take no for an answer. He hung around for so long and bragged about himself so much that Dundee finally gave in, mainly just to shut the kid up.

Willie and Cassius climbed into the ring and began to spar. Cassius quickly measured Pastrano's moves and began slipping jabs and hooks past the big man's defense. Dundee rang the bell and halted the massacre before the old pro got hurt. He was impressed. The kid had some moves, no doubt. "When you turn pro, kid, give me a call." One year, and one gold medal later, Cassius made the call.

Under Angelo Dundee's watchful eye, Cassius made quick strides in his training. Dundee was smart enough to let Cassius fight the way he wanted to. Instead of pushing him, he nudged him. Soon, Cassius was perfecting his skills. His hand speed improved. His foot work was smoother. He was becoming a boxer instead of a fighter.

Cassius fought two more professional bouts in 1960, winning both easily. He bounced four more opponents into retirement in the early months of 1961. After his sixth straight win, Cassius and his team departed for Las Vegas, where he was to fight Duke Sabedong.

During his stay in Las Vegas, Cassius appeared on the *Gorgeous George TV Show*. Gorgeous George was a flamboyant professional wrestler with long blond hair. He also had a quick wit and a dapper style.

But Gorgeous George was no match for the Louisville Lip. Cassius was at his outrageous best. He also made the first of his many predictions. He told George that after their fight, Duke Sabedong would "need a groundhog to deliver his mail. They'll all fall in the round I call."

The fight itself went pretty well as planned. For the most part, Cassius toyed with Sabedong, putting in just enough effort to gain an easy decision.

Secretly, Angelo Dundee and others on Cassius's team were concerned. Cassius was winning, sure, but it was too easy. They needed to find their young phenom an opponent who would wake him up. Cassius needed someone good enough to force him to fight a strategic bout. That wake-up call would come a little earlier than expected.

The Lip's next match was a scheduled ten-rounder against a crafty veteran named Sonny Banks. In the third round, Cassius was caught off guard by a left hook that dropped him to the canvas. It was the first time he had been put down in a bout. He was both angry and embarrassed. He got up and laid a royal pounding on Banks. The tough old lefty fell in a heap at Cassius's feet midway through the fourth round.

Dundee and the boys were pleased. Not only had Cassius finally shown some in-ring emotion, he had also proved he could take a lick or two. The time was right for a real challenge.

The opponent they chose was the "Old Mongoose" himself, Archie Moore. The bout was scheduled for November 15, 1962, in Los Angeles. Hollywood was about to get its first peek at the Louisville Lip.

Cassius was at his poetic best before the fight, putting his first prediction into verse: "I'll say it again, I've said it before / Archie Moore will fall in four."

True to his word, Cassius put the old vet on his backside in the fourth round. Then he went looking for bigger fish to fry. The catch he set his sights on was none other than the current heavyweight champion of the world, Sonny Liston.

The champ had been at ringside for the Moore bout, and Cassius had made a point of hurling verbal garbage at him. "I'm faster than Sonny Liston, younger than Sonny Liston, bigger than Sonny Liston and better than Sonny Liston. He's too ugly to be heavyweight champion."

Cassius fought a good fight in the press, but Liston wasn't about to take up the challenge. In his eyes, Cassius was still a just raw rookie. He didn't think Cassius had earned a place in the ring with a champion of his stature. Sonny Liston refused to accept Cassius's mocking challenge. He suggested the young fighter needed a few more notches on his belt before he was ready to take on the big boys.

So, Cassius and his team set about planning his first title shot. They scheduled a trio of tune-up bouts against opponents with their own unique styles.

Predicting "this ain't no jive, he'll go in five," Cassius demolished southpaw Charlie Powell in Pittsburgh, Pennsylvania, using combinations (a series of jabs, hooks and body shots) and elusive foot speed.

That win set up his next fight with Doug Jones at Madison Square Garden. As the two fighters stood in the ring before the bout, Cassius yelled, "I'm the prettiest. I'm the greatest. I can't be whipped." The crowd was in a frenzy as Cassius eased up to Jones and asked, "How tall are you?"

Jones raised a scarred eyebrow and demanded, "What do you want to know that for?"

Cassius smiled and whispered, "So I'll know how far to step back when I drop you in the fourth."

Cassius's mouth almost cost him the fight. Jones proved to be a lot tougher than Cassius thought. Jones matched him blow for blow and in the eyes of many of the armchair judges, he actually won the bout. When the decision came down in Cassius's favor, there was a near riot at the Garden. Irate fans littered the ring with programs, paper cups, peanuts, paper airplanes, even a switchblade.

Cassius casually bent down, picked up a peanut, cracked the shell, and the ate the nut. Cool, calm and collected, right? Hardly! Cassius knew he had been lucky to come away with a win.

There was another "teacher" waiting in the wings to give Cassius his next lesson. The Clay team went to England where Cassius was to face the British Commonwealth champ, Henry Cooper. Cooper was a tough ex-dockworker with a grizzled face and a temper to match. He was a hard-punching, hard-drinking boxer with a pile-driving right hand that his followers lovingly dubbed "'Enry's 'ammer."

The match took place in front of 55,000 blood-thirsty, beer-fueled fans in famed Wembley Stadium. Cooper took the fight right to Cassius, slamming him with a barrage of thundering shots.

For a while, it appeared the bashing Brit had the upper hand. He even dropped Cassius to the deck late in the fourth round. Cassius was up quickly, but he was stunned by Cooper's powerful punch. When the bell rang, Cassius staggered back to his corner. He needed more than a rest. He needed a miracle.

Luckily for Cassius Clay, he had Angelo Dundee in his corner. The sly trainer had a plan of his own. It was time to play the "stall game." Just as the bell was about to ring for round five, Dundee called the referee over to Cassius's corner. He showed the ref a small tear in Cassius's glove. A tear in a boxing glove could cut and hurt the opposing fighter.

The ref had no choice. He stopped the bout while Dundee and his men repaired Cassius's glove.

When the fight started again, Cassius's head had cleared and he had regained his strength. He leaped to his feet and proceeded to pound Cooper with dazzling lefts and rights. Before the round was over, the referee waved his hands and stopped the bout. Cassius had survived, but just barely.

Now he began lobbying long and loud for a shot at the title. Cassius wanted to fight Sonny Liston. But it's not clear he knew what he would be getting into. Sonny Liston was a violent fighter who seemed to enjoy hurting his opponents. He was the first champ with a prison record. He had been arrested numerous times for assault and drunken behavior.

Liston may have had trouble in the streets, but in the ring, he was the king. His handlers worked long and hard to create a clean, homey image for their fighter. But one look into those eyes, and you got the feeling that this man could kill.

Sonny Liston had watched Cassius's last two fights and he wasn't impressed. He thought Cassius was just another boxer with a big mouth. The champ was sure Cassius couldn't touch him.

Besides, he wanted the chance to seal that Lip shut once and for all. There was only one legal way to do that. And that was to offer Cassius Clay a shot at the heavyweight boxing championship of the world.

Chapter 4

The Birth of Muhammad Ali

To appreciate the importance of the Clay-Liston bout, you have to understand the state of boxing in the early 1960s. This was more than a title fight. It was a battle of good against evil. Just who was good and who was evil depended on your opinion.

When Charles "Sonny" Liston was crowned heavyweight champion of the world on September 25, 1962, the sport was in serious need of a boost.

For much of the 1950s, the International Boxing Clubs (IBC) of New York and Chicago controlled and arranged most of the major bouts. Big Jim Norris of New York and Arthur Wirtz of Chicago were the two men who ruled the roost at the IBC, and they did so with an iron fist. They also controlled the two places where these fights were held, Madison Square Garden in New York and the Chicago Stadium.

It was no secret that the professional boxing world at this time was involved with organized crime. The

United States government began investigating the activities of the Mafia in the 1950s. At that time, they also looked at the IBC.

Most of the Mafia men the investigators spoke to refused to answer any questions. This is known as "taking the fifth," as in the Fifth Amendment of the American constitution. According to that amendment, you don't have to answer any question that might get you into trouble. Although they believed the IBC was involved in crime, the US government couldn't get enough evidence to prove it.

None of the people involved with the IBC would tell what they knew, so the government had to try something else. All the feds had to do was show that the IBC controlled the professional boxing business. If that was true, it made the IBC a monopoly. Monopolies were illegal.

Looking through IBC records, investigators noticed that a promoter by the name of Jack Hurley had filed a protest against Norris. He claimed that Big Jim refused to give a boxer named Kid Matthews a shot at the title, even though he was the top-rated contender. Hurley said, "We never get a chance, because Jim Norris and those people in New York run a nice store and they monopolize everything." Bingo! This was the proof the government needed.

In 1959, Judge Sylvester J. Ryan ruled that the IBC, Norris, and Wirtz were guilty of monopolizing the fight game. Norris was booted out of New York and out of the sport of boxing. He moved to Chicago, where he owned the Chicago Black Hawks, a team in the National Hockey League. In the end, Norris didn't suffer much for his crimes. Instead, it was Norris's cronies, Blinky Palermo and Frankie Carbo, who payed his dues with lengthy stays in federal prison.

Into the middle of this mess stepped Sonny Liston, who just happened to have spent a little time in jail himself. It was there that he had learned to fight, and it was there that he had developed his sledgehammer right hand.

When he got out of jail, Liston became a professional boxer. His contract was handled by Joseph "Bep" Barone, who was to receive 50 per cent of Liston's earnings. In reality, much of Sonny's winnings went directly to a pair of hoodlums in Chicago who were involved with the illegal side of boxing. They were Blinky Palermo and Frankie Carbo.

When the government shut down the IBC, the sport of boxing was given a direct slap in the face. It had a very bad reputation in the public's eye. A star attraction was needed to save the sport. Sonny Liston wanted to be the guy. His connection to the gangsters was kept in the shadows. Instead, he was paraded around as a former felon who had seen the error of his ways and was reformed. Only in America, his agents cried, could a bad man become a good man and reach the top rung on the heavyweight ladder.

Not many experts gave Cassius Clay much of a chance against Liston. Sonny was a powerful fighter. This was the man who flattened Floyd Patterson not once, but twice. At the time, Floyd was the only man ever to hold the heavyweight title twice, but he didn't last five minutes in the ring with Liston. What chance would a loose-lipped punk from Louisville have?

At the second Patterson bout, Cassius tried to steal the spotlight from Liston. He jumped into the ring and went at the champ with all the lip he could muster. Liston listened calmly, then raised a single fist and slowly said, "You're next, big mouth."

It was only one in a series of confrontations between the two before the big fight. Some time later, at a Las Vegas casino, Liston spotted Cassius on the dance floor. He walked up to him and slapped him hard across the face. "That's for being so fresh," he snarled.

Up to this point Cassius had thought all the word games were just that — games. But Sonny Liston had a convict's heart, and it was humorless and cold.

At the weigh-in for the fight, Cassius put on a crazy display that had his followers deeply concerned. He attacked Liston, calling him a big, dumb bear and an old monkey. Cassius boasted that he would "float like a butterfly and sting like a bee." Then he proceeded to fly around the room, shadow boxing and jumping around wildly. All the time, Cassius was yelling that he was "gonna whup the old monkey."

Cassius got so wound up, his blood pressure shot through the roof, climbing above the 200 level. His doctors even wondered if he should be permitted to fight in his condition. Cassius's handlers finally got him out of there in one piece, but not before he was fined $2,500 for his behavior.

Back in his hotel room, Cassius was remarkably calm. He told Angelo Dundee that it was all an act, just a show to scare Liston a little. Cassius said he was at peace with himself, because he had found a new path to follow, and he would begin to walk it after the fight. Dundee wasn't sure what Cassius meant, but he would soon find out.

Shortly before the bout, Cassius had a visitor. Malcolm X, a follower of Elijah Muhammad and the Lost-Found Nation of Islam in the Wilderness, or the Black Muslims as they were often called, came in to give Cassius some pre-fight advice and kind words. He whispered, "This fight is the truth. It's the cross and the crescent fighting in a prize ring — for the first time. It's a modern crusade."

Cassius was well aware of the importance of this fight to the African-American population and to the Nation of Islam. Shortly after the incident at the bridge, Clay had begun to seriously consider the teachings of the Muslim religion. He had always had an interest in it. In fact, he had wanted to write a term paper on the Black Muslims in 1959, but his teacher wouldn't allow him to do it. He couldn't understand why a teacher — a black teacher at that — would not allow him to write about other African-American people. There must be more to this, he thought.

Cassius started to attend Muslim meetings and listen to their sermons. By the time the Liston fight was to take place, Cassius knew as much about Muslim beliefs as many of the men who taught about them. He also knew he was going to become a Muslim.

But Cassius being Cassius, he had to do it in a grand fashion. A week before the big fight, he had gone to New York to meet with the Black Muslim leader, Elijah Muhammad. Cassius promised him that he would become a convert to the Islam after he had disposed of Sonny Liston.

Cassius was a 7-to-1 underdog when he climbed into the ring for his first championship title fight on February 25, 1964. As he stepped between the ropes, he felt something he had never experienced before. He felt fear.

Early in the fight, Cassius moved swiftly around the ring, cutting off the angles that Liston liked to play. He jabbed continuously and forced Liston into swinging wildly, tiring the older boxer. Cassius then started trading body blows with Liston, pounding punch after punch into the ribs and sides of the champ.

By the fourth round, Liston was visibly tired. Near the end of that round, Cassius used a punch he called the "corkscrew" to open up a nasty gash on the champ's face. It was the first time in his career that Liston's weathered old beak had been cut.

Back in his corner, Liston was a damaged fighter. His arms were bruised. His chest ached. As his corner crew rubbed his aching muscles with liniment, Liston knew there was only one way he was going to win this fight.

For much of round five, Liston wasn't too eager to trade punches with Cassius. He was more interested in clutching and grabbing his opponent. In the last seconds of the round, he had Cassius in a virtual bearlock.

After the round, Cassius's eyes began to sting. He felt extreme pain. He begged Dundee to cut off his gloves and throw in the towel. His corner guys figured that some of the powerful liniment Liston's handlers rubbed him down with must have got in Cassius's eyes. That's the "official" story anyway. Dundee just told Cassius to get out there and fight.

He fought the entire round in a daze, with his eyes watering and glazed over. Liston came at him with everything he had. He rifled lefts and rights towards Cassius's head. He pounded Clay's upper torso. Somehow, Cassius survived. After the bout, the referee told the press he had come very close to calling the fight at that point, but the bell saved Cassius.

Later, one of Liston's handlers claimed they had rubbed a secret liniment mixture on Liston's gloves. This was a method they called "juicing the gloves." In reality, it was a last-resort method to grab victory from the jaws of defeat. And it almost worked.

Back in Cassius's corner, his eyes began to clear. By the time the bell rang for the sixth round, he could see just fine. And what he saw was fear in the eyes of Sonny Liston. The champ had nothing left. He had used all the gas in his tank trying to take down Clay in the fifth. There was nothing left but fumes. Cassius took control of the fight, connecting with hard body shots and crisp jabs. That meant bye-bye Sonny Liston.

When the bell rang for round seven, Liston stayed in his corner. He was throwing in the towel. Cassius Clay was the new heavyweight champion of the world.

As usual, Cassius wasn't modest about his achievement. He stepped on the ropes and yelled, "I am the greatest. I told you I'd do it. I done it. I told you. I'm the king of the world."

If Clay's astonishing win was a surprise, then he had a blockbuster to lay on the world the next day at the post-fight press conference.

At the press gathering the day after the fight, Cassius seemed rather quiet. He told the press that he deserved some respect. He wanted the sportswriters to admit he was the greatest boxer in the world. He wanted them to "eat their words." Some of the scribes even went so far as to agree with the Louisville Lip.

Then a reporter asked Cassius if he was a "card-carrying" member of the Black Muslims. Cassius was shocked. It wasn't the press's knowledge of his conversion to Islam that surprised him. It was the reporter's use of the words "card-carrying" that upset him.

"Card-carrying," Clay asked, "what does that mean? We're not communists or nothing, you know. I believe in Allah and I believe in peace." Cassius Clay prepared to make a formal announcement that he was now a Muslim.

Most Americans were shocked at Cassius's decision. Many people thought the Black Muslims were a militant group that could be dangerous. Immediately, the nation was divided about Clay's action. He was either loved or hated. Interestingly, those feelings weren't divided along racial lines. As many blacks as whites were angered that the new champ, an athlete who had brought them so much pride in Rome and joy in Las Vegas, would choose to abandon the Christian faith.

Clay had a quick answer. "It wasn't my choice to be baptized a Christian," he reasoned, "but this, this is my choice."

On Savior's Day, during an event at the Chicago Coliseum, Cassius Clay made his formal announcement. Elijah Muhammad, who until this time had not commented on Clay's decision, now opened his arms to the world champion.

To mark his conversion, Clay wanted to change his name to Cassius X, but that posed a problem. That name would suggest that Clay was a supporter of Malcolm X, and Malcolm was on the way out with the Nation of Islam supporters.

If Clay was going to join Elijah Muhammad, it would have to be under Elijah's terms. Without even consulting Cassius, the Nation of Islam's spiritual leader announced that Cassius Clay was changing his name. Elijah explained that the name "Cassius" lacked a "divine meaning," so he was giving him the name "Muhammad Ali, a name that is his as long as he believes in Allah and follows me. Muhammad means one worthy of praise and Ali is the name of the cousin of the prophet."

Already, it seemed like the newly crowned heavyweight champ and Muslim convert was being tossed around like a political football.

There were other changes, too. Angelo Dundee was replaced as Ali's manager and demoted to trainer only. Hubert Muhammad, Elijah's son, became Ali's new manager. The Louisville Group was dropped.

Ali also began a new training program that reflected his religious beliefs. That meant no alcohol, no smoking, and no pork. It also included regular attendance at Mosque.

Few could argue with Ali's adoption of these restrictions and daily rituals in his personal life, but other beliefs were difficult to accept. Muslims were also forbidden to take part in wars of attrition. The only war Muslims could fight in was one that threatened their religious freedom. This particular belief was to bring Ali a world of trouble.

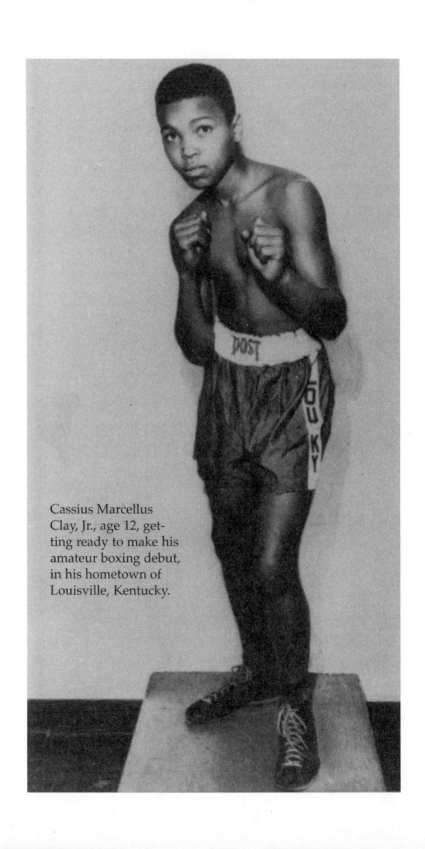

Cassius Marcellus
Clay, Jr., age 12, get-
ting ready to make his
amateur boxing debut,
in his hometown of
Louisville, Kentucky.

Here is Cassius in action at the Rome Olympics in 1960. His opponent is Z. Pietrzykowski of Poland. Cassius defeated the Pole to win the gold medal.

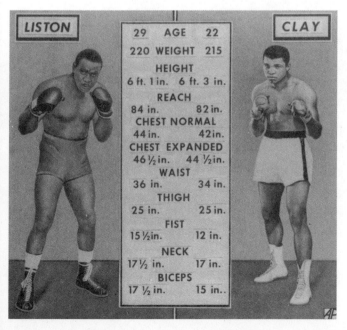

LISTON		CLAY
29	AGE	22
220	WEIGHT	215
	HEIGHT	
6 ft. 1 in.		6 ft. 3 in.
	REACH	
84 in.		82 in.
	CHEST NORMAL	
44 in.		42 in.
	CHEST EXPANDED	
46½ in.		44½ in.
	WAIST	
36 in.		34 in.
	THIGH	
25 in.		25 in.
	FIST	
15½ in.		12 in.
	NECK	
17½ in.		17 in.
	BICEPS	
17½ in.		15 in..

This is how champion Sonny Liston and challenger Cassius Clay measured up for their world heavyweight title bout at Miami Beach, February 25, 1964.

Heavyweight champion Cassius Clay, now known as Muhammad Ali, stands over challenger Sonny Liston, after landing his "phantom punch." The bout on May 25, 1965, only lasted about one minute.

Canadian challenger George Chuvalo covers up as Muhammad Ali launches a flurry of punches. Ali won the fight, which took place in Toronto in March 1966.

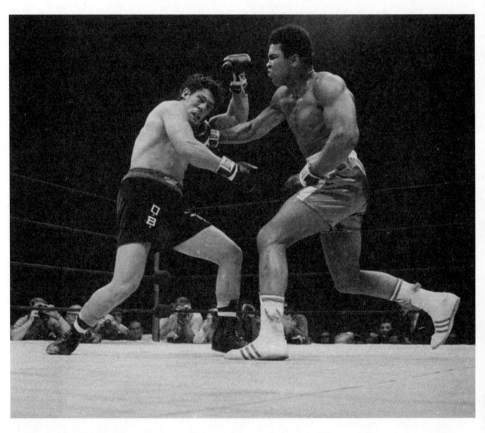

Muhammad Ali pile drives a right to the jaw of Oscar Bonavena of Argentina on December 7, 1970. It was one of Ali's first fights after having his conviction for draft evasion struck down.

Muhammad Ali speaks at a convention of Black Muslims in Chicago in 1968. Seated behind him is Elijah Muhammad, then leader of the Nation of Islam.

Muhammad Ali kisses a child during a visit to an orphanage in San Pedro, Ivory Coast, in 1997. Ali also donated food, wheelchairs and medicine to the orphanage during his goodwill visit.

Chapter 5

The Exile of Muhammad Ali

After his religious conversion, the first order of business for the new champ was a rematch with Sonny Liston. The bout was originally slated for Boston Garden in November, but just three days before the opening bell, Ali collapsed in pain. He was diagnosed with a hernia and was rushed to the hospital for emergency surgery. The bout was rescheduled for May 25, 1965.

While he was recovering, Ali heard that Malcolm X had been assassinated while giving a speech in New York. Ali never expressed any grief publicly over the death of his early Muslim advisor. Muhammad Ali was now a follower of Elijah's Nation of Islam, which had stopped associating with Malcolm X.

Shortly after the shooting, the Massachusetts boxing commission decided it is was too dangerous to stage the Liston-Ali fight in their state. After a lot of searching and intense negotiations, the state of Maine granted the Liston-Ali camps a license to stage the fight there.

The bout would be held in the small town of Lewiston, Maine. The thought of holding a heavy-weight title fight in a 6,000-seat arena, in a town that no one had ever heard of, only added to the bizarre events surrounding the fight. The little town was turned inside out with the arrival of security people, Muslim fundamentalists, and Hollywood celebrities. Even the referee was a celebrity. Jersey Joe Walcott was a former champion of the world. He may have been famous, but events would show that Jersey Joe was out of his element as the third man in the ring.

Ali was all business when he climbed between the ropes. He wanted a quick win and a quicker ride out of the chilly Maine air. Not even Ali could have dreamed how quick it was to be.

From the moment the boxers entered the ring, it became a comedy of errors. Robert Goulet, a slick Las Vegas crooner, forgot the words to the American national anthem. At least he had an excuse. He was a Canadian.

At the opening bell, Ali immediately took the action to Liston. The former champ looked sluggish, allowing Ali to crowd him. Ali landed a quick combination and backed away near the ropes. Liston followed him and threw a wild right hand that left him off balance. Ali slipped a quick piston-like punch to Liston's temple that caught the ex-champ off guard.

That invisible blow became known as the "phantom punch." Filmed footage of it has been dissected and examined as carefully as the Zapruder film that captured the assassination of President John Kennedy. Still, no one is sure what really happened.

Liston slid to the deck and stayed there. The crowd was stunned. Ali stood over him, yelling at him to get back up. But Liston stayed down. Referee Walcott told Ali the count couldn't start until the champ went to his neutral corner. Finally, Ali went to his corner and Walcott began to count to 10, pointing a finger at the fallen Liston for every number he ran off: 1...2...3...

In the confusion, the official timer had already started and was almost finished his count. Slowly, Liston made it to his feet. Walcott checked his eyes, and motioned for the fight to continue. As Ali moved in for the kill, Walcott suddenly turned away and walked to the apron of the ring. Nat Fleischer, the editor of *Ring Magazine,* was shouting his name. He told Walcott that the official timer had finished his count before Liston got up. The fight should be over!

Walcott looked over his shoulder and saw that Ali was thundering left and right hooks into Liston's torso. Walcott ran over, separated the two battlers and raised Ali's arms. The fight was history. It had taken less than a minute. But the debate over what exactly happened in that square ring would go on for years.

As usual, Ali had all the answers. He claimed he saw the so-called phantom punch in a dream. Jack Johnson, the first black heavyweight champion, had come to him and showed him how to use the surprise blow to his advantage. Johnson called it the "anchor punch," Ali said. Most boxing purists had other names for it. Some called it the fix. Others called it the dive. They suspected Liston had let Muhammad Ali win.

After weeks of investigations and hearings by both the F.B.I. and boxing executives, there was still no evidence that Liston had taken a dive. Shortly before his death in 1969, Liston told a reporter, "I lost that fight because Nat Fleischer said I lost that fight." When asked to explain how that was possible, Liston answered, "Because he could count to ten faster than Jersey Joe Walcott."

The re-match and Ali's successful defense brought an end to the first half of Clay-Ali's career. From here, he was on a fast track to fame and fortune.

Ali's next defense of the title was against Floyd Patterson, who was trying to become the only fighter to regain the heavyweight belt for a third time.

The lead-up to the fight quickly escalated into a war of words, many of them biting and mean. There was no humor in this war. Ali called Patterson the "Black-White Hope," proclaiming that the former champ was a chump who marched to the white man's drum. Patterson replied that Clay — Patterson refused to use Ali's "Muslim name" — was a disgrace to America and the American negro.

There may have been no clear winner in the war of words, but there certainly was one in the boxing ring. On November 22, 1965, Ali pounded Patterson into submission, yapping at him the whole time. Patterson was in such pain that he later admitted he wished Clay had finished him off sooner. The end came in the 12th round and Patterson's career as a major contender was over.

In 1966, Ali defended his crown five times, easily destroying his opponents. He was surprised by the hard chin of Canadian heavyweight champ George Chuvalo, but he still battered him for 15 rounds. A rematch with Briton Henry Cooper was next. Ali axed him in six rounds. Brian London fell in three, Karl Mildenberger in twelve, and Cleveland Williams in three. Ali opened 1967 in similar fashion, winning a decision over Ernie Terrell before flattening Zora Folley in seven.

While the Ali express was rolling along smoothly inside the ring, life was getting pretty complicated outside the safety of the square circle. Ali went through a messy divorce when his wife refused to accept his religious conversion. He was also fighting with the US government, which was trying to draft him into the US Army to fight in Vietnam.

In the USA at the time, every male citizen under the age of 30 not in college and with reasonable intelligence could be called to join the army. At first, Ali appeared to be safe. It seemed he wasn't of "reasonable intelligence." He failed his first two army intelligence tests, scoring so poorly the military rated his I.Q. as a lowly 79, well below the average 100. Some writers were skeptical about Ali's performance. He could fight with his fists in a ring, but he was too dumb to fight with a gun?

The Vietnam War was controversial. Many believed America had to fight to keep the communists from taking over the small Asian country. Others believed the US should not be involved in a foreign war.

Ali was outspoken on the subject, as usual. He said, "I got nothin' against them Viet Congs." Ali had been poorly treated in his own country because of his race. African Americans had their own battles to fight in the USA. He saw no reason to fight people in another country whom he'd never met, and who had never done him any harm. Besides, fighting in the Vietnam War would conflict with his religious beliefs.

Late in 1966, the army dropped the level of scores needed to pass its I.Q. test. The new rules meant that Ali passed the test. He was now eligible for the army. No man could beat him in the ring, but he was about to fight a losing battle in the courtroom.

On April 28th, 1967, Ali announced that he was refusing to serve in the army because his Muslim faith prevented him from fighting wars of attrition. His religious beliefs were unshakable, he said, and Allah was protecting him. That argument wasn't accepted in the courtroom.

On June 25th, Ali was stripped of his heavyweight title and sentenced to five years in prison for refusing to sign his U.S. Army induction papers. Through his lawyers, Ali posted bail and appealed the ruling. He managed to stay out of jail, but he was unable to fight. He lost his ability to earn a living to provide for his family. His legal bills were piling up. Ali was forced to accept work giving speeches and doing television commercials.

In these years, Ali was at an age and stage where he was in prime condition for boxing. His legal problems meant he missed out on what would have been the best years of his boxing career. Had he been allowed to fight in those years, he probably would have earned over 10 million dollars, which would equal about 100 million dollars in today's money.

For most of his first two years in exile from the boxing ring, Muhammad Ali was criticized for refusing to fight for his country. Some of his fans blamed his involvement with the Nation of Islam. Others felt he was a coward to take their money but not fight for their liberty. Ali remained steadfast. It was not his war, he explained. It was not even America's war.

Ali did receive support from some rather unexpected sources. Sir Bertrand Russell, a noted British philosopher and a knighted Member of the British Empire, wrote Ali a letter that expressed support for Ali's stand.

"In the coming months there is no doubt that the men who rule Washington will try to damage you in every way open to them," Russell wrote, "but I am sure you know you spoke for your people and for the oppressed everywhere in the courageous defiance of American power. You have my wholehearted support."

By the time Ali received Sir Bertrand's letter, he was a convicted felon and his passport had been taken back. The very same thing had happened to Bertrand Russell during World War I. Ali's passport problems began when he tried to arrange a bout in Tokyo. When the US government heard of Ali's Asian vacation, they cancelled his passport. How did they know of Ali's plans? They had his phone tapped so that they could listen in on his private conversations.

As it turned out, Ali's anti-war stand didn't fall on deaf ears. The youth of America were listening. There were monthly, sometimes daily, peace marches in every major American city. Thousands of young men were either burning their draft cards or fleeing to Canada or Sweden to avoid being drafted into the army.

Meanwhile, a rough and rumble, street-wise brawler from Philadelphia had grabbed Ali's vacant heavyweight throne. Smokin' Joe Frazier had never had the opportunity to fight Ali. But in his absence, he was beating all the competition.

Frazier had already successfully defended his heavyweight champion title four times when the Supreme Court of the Southern District Federal Court overturned Ali's conviction on refusing induction on June 20, 1970. That decision opened the door for Ali's return to competitive boxing. He still had to apply for a license and each individual state could decide to turn down his request. But at least there was hope.

Setting up fights was one problem. Another was Ali's fitness to fight. The former champ was in no shape to make a quick comeback. Ali had grown soft during his three years away from boxing. It would take many months of tough road work and countless hours in the gym before Ali would be ready to step into the ring against a top challenger.

As expected, Ali found that he was still being blacklisted by many states. State after state and commission after commission refused to grant Ali a boxing license. Finally, after weeks of searching, an opponent and a location were found. Ali would return to action against Jerry Quarry in Atlanta on October 26, 1970. Quarry was a seasoned pro who had lost a unanimous decision to Jimmy Ellis in 1967 in one of the many fights staged to crown a successor to Ali.

The road to Ali's return to fighting wasn't smooth. Death threats were made against him and his family.

This was nothing new. On the night Malcom X was murdered in 1965, a bomb exploded near Ali's apartment. Although the police were sure there was no connection between the two events, Ali and his followers weren't so confident. Quickly, the Ali entourage hired a pair of bulky security guards to watch over the champ.

There was even a bomb threat made on Ali's home moments before his match against Quarry was to begin. But, in true Hollywood fashion, the show went on. With an assortment of the famous and the fashionable looking on, Muhammad Ali completed his comeback with a workman-like effort against Quarry. By the end of the third round, Quarry's face resembled a mine pit, and his corner wisely decided to throw in the towel.

While it's true that Ali looked out of step and out of shape in his first return bout, his new fighting strategy paid dividends. Instead of attacking, he stayed on the perimeter. He danced and ducked around Quarry. Then, without warning, he would step into the middle of the ring and snap off a razor-quick jab. While it looked odd, it definitely worked. Quarry had the scars to prove it.

The next stop on the Ali comeback tour was set for Madison Square Garden in December. His opponent was Oscar Bonavena, who decided to insult the former champ by calling him a "big, black kangaroo." In the ring, the big Argentine leaned over and whispered in Ali's ear, "You a chicken. Why you no fight for your country?"

Clearly, Bonavena wanted to get Ali so worked up his anger would overtake his concentration. For a while, it worked. Ali was taking more punches than he was dishing out, and the big South American was hugging, holding, grasping, and grabbing at every chance. Finally, in the 15th round, Ali broke free and smoked a hook that dented Bonavena's chin. The Argentinian dropped like an anvil, thumping to the mat with a sickening thud.

While the referee was still counting him out, Ali grabbed the ringside microphone and shouted to the crowd, "Where's that big Joe Frazier? I did what he couldn't do ... I knocked out Bonavena. Where's Joe Frazier? I want Joe Frazier."

There's an old cliché that says, "Be careful what you wish for, because you will surely get it." Ali was going to get Frazier. And when it was over, it's doubtful he would admit to ever having wanted him.

Many armchair athletes felt Ali wasn't ready to take on Frazier. The experts who had been following Frazier's blazing path were *certain* Ali wasn't ready. With only two fights in three years, Ali would need all his experience and more than a little luck to withstand the Philly Flash's explosive attack.

Joe Frazier was born in Beauport, South Carolina. His father was a dirt-poor farmer who was better known for his moonshine than his peaches and sweet potatoes. In an attempt to escape the poverty that surrounded him, young Joe Frazier moved to the city of Philadelphia. He found work as a butcher's apprentice and began to train as a boxer.

In the 1976 movie *Rocky*, a boxing rookie named Rocky Balboa trains by pounding punches into a slab of beef hung in a meat cooler. That scene was based on Joe Frazier. That's the way Smokin' Joe used to barbeque his meat — with Smokin' left hooks.

Like Ali, Frazier was an Olympic gold-medal winner. He grabbed gold for the USA at the 1964 Games in Tokyo. Frazier hadn't even expected to compete. He made the team as an alternate and was thrown into battle when Buster Mathis broke a knuckle in training and couldn't compete.

Frazier waltzed through his three preliminary fights, but had to battle to win the gold over German bus driver Hans Huber. It wasn't that Huber was a better boxer. It's just that Frazier had a broken hand at the time. That made his task a bit tougher. But he did it, and he never mentioned the broken hand.

Frazier was upset that he didn't receive the same hero's welcome that the American public gave Cassius Clay (Ali) when he came home with the gold in 1960. Sure, Philadelphia loved him, but the whole country loved Clay. Even years later, those bitter feelings remained. When asked about Ali's appearance at the

1996 Olympic Games in Atlanta, Frazier snarled, "It should have been me. Why not me? I'm a good American. When am I gonna get my due? I could have run up there like a real champion. I'm still in shape." It was that same attitude that Frazier would carry into the ring with him when he fought Ali.

There was some difficulty in arranging that fight. While both parties were willing to butt heads and go at it, Ali was still a boxer in exile. Luckily, the state of New York finally agreed to license the bout.

The "fight of the century" was scheduled for March 8, 1971, in boxing's "palace of pugilism," Madison Square Garden. It would feature the biggest purse in the history of boxing. Each fighter would bring home a guaranteed multimillion-dollar paycheck.

To add to the drama, Ali composed a little ditty to assure his followers that he hadn't lost the gift of gab: "It might shock ya and amaze ya /But I'm gonna retire Smokin' Joe Frazier."

In front of a packed house and a world-wide audience, Ali showed a new determination. He went after Frazier with clever footwork and masterful defense. In the early going, Ali unleashed the "Ali Shuffle," a toe-tapping, jitterbug-type dance that had Frazier confused and off balance. When they did journey to the center of the ring, the damage was severe. Both men took several solid shots that would have dropped lesser fighters.

Ali was in control in the early rounds, but Frazier took total control of the middle rounds. He battered Ali with an impressive display of punching power. Frazier chalked up a considerable lead on most of the ringside scorecards.

Ali made a strong comeback in round 14, but he couldn't find the energy to deliver what he desperately needed: a knockout punch. When the final bell rang, all the votes went in Frazier's favor. Smokin' Joe stayed the champ, and Muhammad Ali suffered the first loss of his professional career.

Ali did score a major victory of his own less than three months later. On June 28, 1971, in a landmark decision, the Supreme Court of the United States overturned Ali's 1967 conviction, ruling he had been drafted illegally. Now the former champ could box anywhere. He would be able to get enough fights under his belt to prepare him for another challenge for the heavyweight crown.

Chapter 6

The Greatest

Over the next twenty months, Ali fought and won an amazing ten bouts, five of them by knockout. Some familiar names such as Chuvalo, Patterson, and Quarry fell to the returning King of the Ring. The others were an assortment of pugs, thugs, and mugs that would be all but forgotten if they hadn't lost to Ali.

Plans were almost finalized for a return bout with Frazier when Ali stepped into the ring to face a former marine named Ken Norton. A stern-looking goliath with a sculptured physique, Norton was unimpressed by Ali's record, his politics, and his methods. He was ready to rumble.

Maybe Ali took the massive marine too lightly. Maybe his focus was on the Frazier rematch. Whatever the reason, Ali was unprepared for Norton, whose only style was that he had no style. What he did have was a right hand that could crack concrete. Unfortunately for Ali, his jaw was made of flesh and bone. When Norton landed a howitzer on Ali's chin midway through the match, he cracked Ali's jaw like a thin wedge of well-aged plywood.

Despite the throbbing agony, Ali desperately fought on. Every punch he threw sent a spasm like an electrical shock up his spine. Every time he connected, he almost passed out from the pain.

But Ali went the distance, and he almost won. In a split decision, Norton got the win and Ali suffered his second loss. More important, his broken jaw would need a long recovery period, and time was ticking away for the 31-year-old former champion.

Amazingly, Ali's jaw healed much quicker than anticipated. He was ready to resume full training only two months after Norton's right hand re-arranged his profile. The opening item on Ali's agenda was a pair of warm-up bouts to get back in shape for a rematch with Joe Frazier.

Ali went back into the ring with Ken Norton on September 10, 1973. Once again, Norton proved to be a tough customer. Ali was sluggish in the early rounds, but he found his range just in time to escape with a split decision. Still, to many of the experts at ringside, it could have gone either way.

Ali's next bout didn't exactly prove that he was ready to take on Frazier either. Ali met Rudi Rubbers, the Dutch national champ, in Jakarta, Indonesia. Rubbers bounced all around the ring, never straying too close to Ali's sizzling jabs. Although Ali won with a unanimous decision, it was clear he wasn't near where he would have to be to extinguish Smokin' Joe's heat.

When observers noted that Ali threw only six right-handed punches during the entire bout, the former champ admitted he was saving his right hand for Frazier. He had some bone chips in the hand and he needed to rest his hurting hams before taking them out against Iron Joe.

The rematch wouldn't have quite the same hype as the earlier bout. Frazier was no longer the champ. He had lost his title to George Foreman in September 1973. Still, the Ali-Frazier bout set a new standard, with the largest purse in pro boxing history — $5,000,000.

This time Ali was prepared for Frazier, both mentally and physically. He knew he had lost some of his punching power, so he decided to out-run and out-gun Smokin' Joe. Ali spent more time doing road work than he did in the gym.

This new dedication paid off when the two entered the ring on January 28, 1974. Ali completely outclassed Frazier, spinning him in circles with constant motion. Just when Frazier felt he had Ali tied up on the ropes, Ali would spin away, slip into the middle of the ring, and throw a little water on Smokin' Joe's fire.

By the end of the match, Frazier's face was a mass of bumps and bruises. Even Ali looked like he had been spiked with slabs of stone. But he gladly traded his now-ugly mug for a career-reviving victory and another chance at reclaiming his heavyweight crown.

Ali was now the top-ranked contender for the heavyweight title. Plans for a Foreman-Ali title fight were just being made when a new figure appeared on the scene. His name was Don King, and the boxing world had never seen anyone like him. The new promoter was a former felon and convicted murderer with a corkscrew afro hairdo and a sense of bravado that made Ali seem meek in comparison.

King proposed a plan that was, on paper at least, as bizarre as he looked. King's idea was to hold the Foreman-Ali fight in the African country of Zaire, now known as Congo. The country's president, Mobutu Sese Seko, was eager to show off his country. He said he would put up all the money and provide free accommodations for the boxers, their families, and staff.

Don King promised to deliver a $10,000,000 purse and an "out of this world" television contract. He estimated that one billion people would watch the event. Using an old show business adage, King promised to sell the sizzle, not the steak. That meant hype, hype, and more hype, with loads of money up front before the fight even took place.

Naturally, the Ali and Foreman camps were hesitant at first. Boxing promoters are not known for their honesty. But when Don King dropped $400,000 in cash at their feet, the fight was a go. It was set for September 24, 1974, in Kinshasa, Zaire.

When Ali arrived in Kinshasa for the "Rumble in the Jungle," he was greeted like royalty. Ali got the locals in the palm of his hand by showing a genuine interest in their culture, their language, and their troubles. He was adopted like a son and treated like a king.

George Foreman, on the other hand, was out of his element. He arrived with a crew of bodyguards and a pack of German shepherd dogs for protection. Foreman and his camp stayed away from the Zairean people and made little effort to understand their ways.

Eight days before the bout, Foreman was badly cut above the eye during a sparring session. The fight had to be postponed while his eye healed. Foreman and his camp packed up and returned to America, but Ali stayed put. He continued to train and make new friends in his adopted country.

He also got his body used to Zaire's climate and atmosphere. The fight was to take place at six o'clock in the morning in a massive open-air soccer stadium. The odd time was arranged so the fight could be shown on television during prime time in the USA. Ali set his training schedule around that tip-off time. He awoke at 4 o'clock every morning to meditate and recite his prayers to Allah. Then he began his endless training runs.

Thousands of children would gather along the roadside waiting for Ali to jog by. He would joke with them, talk to them, and preach to them. His message was, "Ali is the greatest. Ali is the greatest. Ali will kill George Foreman. Ali — *Bomaye*! Ali — *Bomaye*!" *Bomaye* is a Swahili word meaning "kill." When Foreman and his followers returned to Zaire, he found he wasn't going to fight just Ali. He was going to have to fight an entire country!

Except for his new friends in Zaire, no one was giving Ali much of a chance against Foreman. George Foreman was another Olympic gold-medal winner for the USA. He had been the surprise winner of the gold at the 1968 Olympic Games in Mexico City. With only 18 amateur fights in his resumé (compared with Ali's 108 amateur fights) when he went to Mexico, he became the first American since 1956 to win the gold on a knockout. When Soviet heavyweight Jonas Cepulis hit the deck, millions of Americans cheered.

These were the same Olympic Games that saw some African-American athletes wear armbands and black gloves on the medal podium to protest the racial inequality that existed in the United States. However, when Foreman won his gold, he paraded around the ring waving an American flag.

Foreman was, and is, a giant of a man. Today you can see him on television commercials cheerfully selling a device for grilling food. Back in the early 1970s, he was a fierce fighter with a snarl that could peel paint. And he could punch. He had destroyed the two boxers who had defeated Ali. It had taken Foreman only five minutes to flatten Joe Frazier and four minutes to knock out Ken Norton. If Ali was going to have a chance against this monster, he would need a plan. As usual, he had one all worked out.

In the opening moments of the brawl, both men were cautious. Then Foreman closed in. He trapped Ali against the ropes, thundering lefts and rights into the ex-champ's mid-section. Unbelievably, Ali made no attempt to move off the ropes. He stayed pinned against the ropes, absorbing incredible punishment. This went on for five rounds, with Foreman pounding Ali's body at will.

In the sportswriters' section, the cigar-chomping scribes were in agreement: it was only a matter of time before this one would be in the books. But one ancient observer knew exactly what Ali was doing.

"Gentleman Jim Corbett," he said.

"What was that, old-timer?" a reporter asked.

"Gentleman Jim Corbett," he repeated. "Ol' Jim used this tactic. Never failed." The aged analyst noted that Foreman wasn't getting in any head shots. He told the boys to watch the ropes. They were looser than usual and Ali was curling up deep in the pocket they created. He predicted Ali was going to let Foreman punch himself out, then storm in for the kill.

Those comments were met with shrugs and laughs. But two rounds later, it was clear the joke was on them. And Foreman.

By round eight of this rumble, Foreman could barely lift his arms. He had thrown hundreds of punches, but had inflicted very little damage on Ali. Then the Muslim master went to work. Ali sprayed jabs, hooks, and combinations at Foreman. With the entire stadium on their feet howling, "Ali — *Bomaye!* Ali — *Bomaye!*" he closed in on his staggering prey.

As Foreman tried in vain to clutch and grab, Ali submarined a thundering hook that caught Foreman flush under the chin. The force of the blow seemed to actually lift the soon-to-be-dethroned champion of the world off his feet. Foreman crashed to the canvas with a resounding thud that seemed to shake the entire stadium. With a nearly full African moon smiling down on him, Muhammad Ali was once again the "King of the World."

In later discussions about the Rumble in the Jungle, Ali denied that his famed "rope-a-dope" was a pre-planned ploy. But we do know that during his pre-fight training sessions, Ali wanted his sparring partners to belt him with body shots. He also spent a great deal of time flopping into the ropes and bouncing back off them.

A magician rarely reveals his tricks, but one thing was certain. Ali proved that muscle and might are poor partners unless they are matched with a keen mind. Ali simply out-thought Foreman. By doing so, he became only the second boxer ever to regain his heavyweight title.

After a short rest and vacation, Ali made three quick defenses of his crown. He defeated Chuck Wepner and Ron Lyle in Las Vegas with TKOs (technical knock-outs). Then he flew halfway around the world for a bout with Joe Bugner in Malaysia. Bugner was a battering ram with a face of stone, but Ali subdued him long enough to win a unanimous 15-round victory.

After this trio of fights, Ali prepared for another international display of pugilism. Once again, promoter Don King was at the controls, pulling all the strings. This time the fight would take place in Manila, capital of the Philippines. It would be the re-match between Joe Frazier and Muhammad Ali.

Dubbed the "Thrilla in Manila," it lived up to its name. To this day, it remains one of the most thrilling — and violent — displays of fighting ever. These two adversaries, who never have and probably never will like each other, stood in the middle of the ring for 15 rounds and pounded each other into submission.

One of the more disturbing things about this fight was the odd behavior of the newly re-crowned champ. Ali attacked Frazier at every opportunity, calling him an "ugly old monkey" and "an ape." He carried a plastic gorilla around wherever he went. He would enter a room and bellow, "Anybody seen Joe Frazier? Where's the gorilla? From Manila? He ain't the champ. He's the chump." When asked for a poetic prediction, Ali broke into a moon-shaped smile and declaimed, "It will be a killa and a chilla and a thrilla when I get that gorilla in Manila."

Difficulties in Ali's personal life at this time may have been the reason behind his lack of respect for Frazier. Ali was having problems in his marriage. He made them worse by travelling to Manila with a "special friend" whom he introduced to President Marcos and the international press as his wife. When all the daily newspapers across the USA plastered a picture of the champ and his "wife" on the front page, the real Mrs. Ali wasn't impressed. She flew to Manila, flew into a rage, then flew back home to begin divorce proceedings.

It was another out-of-the-ring black eye for Ali. Many newspapers around the world were more than happy to take a shot at Ali's character, religion, and lack of respect for his wife.

The action in the ring was unaffected by the controversy. Ali and Frazier just stood there and threw punch after punch. After 14 tiring rounds, a battered and beaten Frazier was unable to meet the bell for the last round. The greatest slugfest in boxing was over. After the match, Ali confessed that he was "as close to death as I could imagine."

Many observers believe this fight did more damage to Ali, both mentally and physically, than any other trip into the ring. Perhaps if he had retired following this match, Ali would have been spared the physical torture he would suffer later in his life. But Ali had two former wives to support — and a third on the way. He had four children to provide for. He had a large team of trainers, doctors, and business partners to pay. So, Ali continued to fight.

Chapter 7

Decline, Defeat, Disgrace

Over the next two years, Muhammad Ali successfully defended his crown six more times, mostly against unknown, but up-and-coming opponents. Jean-Pierre Coopman fell in five. Jimmy Young made it through the scheduled 15 rounds, but all three judges gave the victory to Ali. Richard Dunn was done like dinner in five rounds. Ken Norton proved once again that he could match the champ blow-for-blow, but Ali won an easy decision.

Ali's next two fights, against Alfredo Evangelista and Earnie Shavers, only proved that the champ was getting old, weary, and sloppy. It was clear that his punches lacked pop and power. Many of his handlers begged him to retire as champ, but Ali needed one more payday.

Reluctantly, his advisors agreed. After all, his next opponent was a nobody by the name of Leon Spinks. An odd-looking fellow, Spinks was described by one boxing writer as being "not the sharpest knife in the drawer." But whatever Spinks may have lacked in brains, he made up for in brawn.

On February 15, 1978, in Las Vegas, Nevada, the boxing world stood slack-jawed as they watched Leon Spinks batter an old and overweight Muhammad Ali for 15 agonizing rounds. Most experts hoped that Ali was just waiting for Spinks to wilt before bursting out with a barrage of blasts that would put the pretender out of work.

But it never happened. Ali had nothing to offer. His legs were gone. His spirit was gone. He merely slapped at Spinks, and when the final bell rang, the entire arena fell silent. Muhammad Ali was now a former champ again.

Against everyone's advice, Ali immediately appealed for a re-match, and it was quickly granted. Seven months later, a surprisingly agile Ali entered the ring in New Orleans and completely out-matched Leon Spinks.

Using all his guile and gusto, Ali shuffled, shook, and shimmied away from Spinks's punches. Ali was wise enough to realize his punches couldn't break a pane of glass, so he out-danced and out-thought Spinks to win a unanimous decision.

The win made boxing history. Ali was the first — and still the only — man to wear the heavyweight crown on three separate occasions. To the relief of everyone connected to the champion, Ali announced on June 27, 1979, that he was hanging up the gloves for good.

Unfortunately, life outside the ring wasn't as much fun for Ali as life inside it. He couldn't get used to retirement. He missed the cheering fans. Money, fame, family, and friends were not enough. Ali needed action. He got it when he signed up to fight Larry Holmes in Las Vegas on October 2, 1980.

Perhaps Ali felt Holmes deserved the shot. He had been a faithful sparring partner for the champ, and had often been the victim of Ali's slicing sarcasm.

If Ali felt he owed Holmes something, Holmes certainly made his former boss pay. The whole evening was a disaster for Ali. Holmes toyed with him for the entire fight. After the tenth round, Ali slumped to his stool his head bowed, his lungs gasping for air. He turned to his faithful corner crew and muttered, "It's over." For the first time in his storied career, Ali failed to finish a fight on his feet.

To this day, Ali's closest friend and confidante is photographer Howard Bingham. Bingham has recorded the career of "The Greatest" since 1964. As usual, he was at ringside for the Holmes fight, and he believes it was this brutal bout that caused many of the physical problems that would plague Ali in the 1990s.

In an interview with *Sports Illustrated* in 1998, Bingham remembered that Ali was in great shape that night. He had just come from the Mayo Clinic, where he was given a clean bill of health. He did have a touch of the flu, but his mind was sharp and his reflexes were quick. But just before the fight, Ali took some medication, and he had an adverse reaction to the dosage. In the ring, his eyes were not focused.

What concerned Bingham the most was the fact the champ didn't — maybe couldn't — sweat. "He wasn't perspiring, he wasn't fighting," Bingham recalled. "It doesn't make any sense." What he didn't know then, what no one could have really known then, was that Ali was already planning his next comeback.

It's difficult to understand why Muhammad Ali, a proud and courageous athlete, would decide to fight again after his miserable defeat by Larry Holmes. But Ali decided to try yet another comeback. Against his doctor's advice, Ali signed on to fight Trevor Berbick in a bout scheduled to take place on December 11, 1981, in Nassau.

Berbick wasn't a bad fighter, but he had no right to be in the same ring with Ali. Perhaps the fight officials thought the same way. They scheduled the fight as a 10-rounder. The last time Ali fought a bout scheduled for fewer than 12 rounds, he was 20 years younger and 20 pounds lighter.

It still saddens many of Ali's fans to recall the events of that December evening. When he parted the ropes and rolled into the ring, he looked overweight, bloated, and sickly. Ali managed to stay on his feet, but that was all. When the final curtain came down, Ali waved a limp glove and disappeared into his dressing room.

At least there would be no more pretending. Even if he had wanted another kick at the boxing can, it's doubtful that any state would have permitted another Ali fight. In December 1981, he finally retired for good with a record of 56 wins — 37 of them by knockout — and 5 losses.

Chapter 8

Ambassador to the World

Boxing can be a dangerous sport. Fighters have been seriously injured and even killed in the ring. Strict regulations are needed to protect the boxer's health. Some have gone so far as to suggest the sport be banned. Part of that concern arises from the fate of "The Greatest," Muhammad Ali.

In the mid-1980's, after his retirement, Muhammad Ali began to display frightening physical problems. Suddenly, almost without warning, Ali started shaking uncontrollably. He lost the ability to move his right hand and parts of his face. He also lost much of his vocal power.

At first it was believed Muhammad Ali had developed Parkinson's Disease, a disorder of the nervous system that usually afflicts older people. Recently, Ali's doctors have concluded that the former champ suffers from a condition called Parkinson's Syndrome. He doesn't appear to have the disease itself but suffers many of the same problems of the people who do.

It has not been proven that Muhammad Ali's ailments are the result of brain damage caused by the years of battering in the ring. However, his illness has caused many to wonder about the long-term effects of being slugged repeatedly in the head.

Whatever the cause of his condition, many were shocked by the changes in the former champ when he made occasional public appearances after his retirement from the ring.

But the impression that the once-famed "Louisville Lip" lives like an expressionless mute couldn't be further from the truth. Rather than surrender to his physical problems, Ali has become more active than ever. When the great American boxer Joe Louis was living, he was called "America's Guest." Today, Muhammad Ali is known as "America's Honored Guest." He has been honored from India to Indonesia and Australia to Asia.

And Ali works for these honors. His appearances draw tens of thousands of fans. All of them are more than willing to empty their wallets for a charitable cause if it means having the chance to see a living legend, the man they still call "The Greatest."

Ali is an avid ambassador for racial equality. He travels the world to bring attention to hunger and poverty. He has raised millions of dollars to fight disease in developing countries. He has started countless foundations to help eliminate the ghettos in United

States cities. He has established charities in his name to ensure that every child has clean water to drink, a bed to sleep in, and enough food to eat. Impossible tasks, perhaps, but Ali, his wife, and his followers never stop trying to make the dreams come true.

One of the greatest honors to be bestowed upon Ali was the one that brought him back to the world's attention. Although he was very active in numerous charitable pursuits, few people had seen him since he became ill. In 1996, in front of one of the largest audiences in television history, Muhammad Ali lit the Olympic Flame to begin the 1996 Summer Olympic Games in Atlanta.

After that, there was still one more award for Ali to receive. Ali was presented with a gold medal to replace the one he had tossed into the Ohio River on that muggy day back in 1960. Although he never really left, Muhammad Ali was back.

60 Minutes, the popular news program produced by CBS Television, did a moving and remarkable piece on Ali and his fourth wife, Lonnie. Although he walked slowly and shook slightly, he still had that sly smile. Mrs. Ali assured the world that her husband may appear to be frail, but he is still sharp and focused mentally.

Ali will continue to use his fame to help those less lucky than he is. Today, Muhammad Ali and his wife live quietly on his farm in Berrien Springs, Michigan, surrounded by his seven daughters and two sons. He is still "The Greatest."

Glossary of Boxing Terms

amateur — a person who does something without being paid for it. In boxing, amateur fights are three rounds long. There are as many as five judges. Both boxers wear head protection, usually a leather helmet that protects the face and head from cuts.

bout — see "fight".

boxer — Boxers are classified according to their weight. There are 17 weight classes, ranging from straw-weight (105 to 108 pounds/47.5 to 49 kilograms), to welterweight (147 to 153 pounds/67 to 69.5 kilograms), to heavyweight (over 190 pounds/86 kilograms). There are no limits on how much a heavyweight can weigh.

card — the schedule for a night of fighting. The most important fight is held last and is called the "headline bout." The other fights are called the "undercard."

corner — an area of the ring assigned to a boxer to which he returns at the end of each round. His trainers place a small stool in the corner for the boxer to sit on. The trainers can give their fighter water and whatever attention he may need when he is in his corner between rounds.

corner, neutral — the corner diagonally across from the boxer's home corner. When a fighter is knocked down, the other boxer must go to his neutral corner. The referee will not start counting until that happens.

draw — boxing match in which there is no clear winner.

drop one's guard — to be unprepared for an attack, or to stop defending oneself.

fight — a boxing match. Also called a "bout." A fight can be anywhere from 3 to 12 rounds long. Until 1986, most pro fights were 15 rounds long. Due to concern over the health and welfare of the fighters this was changed to 12 rounds. Olympic bouts are three rounds long. Each state or province has its own boxing commission. That means they usually have their own rules about how a winner is determined. In most pro fights held today, the **"three-knockdown"** rule is in effect, which means that a boxer cannot be knocked down more than three times in a single round. There is also the phrase, **"saved by the bell."** This means that if a boxer is down and the bell rings to signal the end of the round before he is back up, he can continue to fight. Again, depending on where the fight is taking place, different rules can be used.

Golden Gloves — award given when an amateur boxer wins his state championship.

hook — a sweeping punch with a full wind-up that packs a wallop. When it comes from the side, it is designed to land on the temple or side of the jaw. When it comes from below, it is designed to hit the chin. Because it is a long punch, it is easy to see, Therefore, a boxer usually "sets up" the hook with a series of jabs. While the other boxer is trying to defend himself, the offensive boxer will slip in the hook.

jab — a snapping type of punch that is more like a sharp flick than a full punch. It is quick and hard to defend. It usually doesn't have a lot of power behind it so it is used to set up other punches.

judge — person who decides who wins or loses a boxing match. At ringside, there are three judges who score the fight. Most fights don't end with a knockout, so the judges are very important. Each round is scored separately. Most pro fights use a **10-point "must" system** of scoring. That means the winner of the round must be given 10 points. The loser of the round is given anywhere from 1 to 9 points. The judges award points for punches thrown, punches landed, and how the boxer has controlled the round. If all three judges have the same boxer as the winner, it is called a **unanimous decision**. If only two judges have the same boxer as the winner, it is called a **split decision**. If there is no clear winner, the fight is declared a **draw**. The judges can only take away points when ordered to by the referee. Points can be taken from a fighter for fouls such as a **low blow** (a punch below the waist), biting and scratching, holding or tripping, or refusal to obey the orders of the referee.

knockout (KO) — a punch that knocks down a boxer for a count of 10. If the boxer who has been knocked down cannot get up before the referee counts to 10, the opponent wins and is given credit for a knockout or KO.

low blow — a punch below the belt.

match — see "fight".

referee — the third person in the boxing ring. He controls the fight. He makes sure both boxers are fighting within the rules. He keeps the action moving. He also decides if a fighter is too hurt to continue. The referee can also stop the fight for a moment. This is called the **freeze.** When a fighter is cut, the referee can freeze the bout, and consult with the ringside doctor on whether he thinks the fighter can continue to box. The referee can also freeze the bout to give a boxer who has been hit with a low blow time to recover.

ring — area bounded by ropes where a boxing match takes place. The ring is actually a raised and roped-off square 12 x 24–foot (3.66 x 7. 32–metre) platform. The floor is cushioned and has "give." That means the boxers can actually bounce a little on it. Why is this square area called a ring? When boxing first started in the 1800s, it was illegal. Boxers fought with their bare fists, and the fight would not be over until one of them could not continue. There was no designated fighting area. Fans would surround the boxers and form a ring around the fighters. If a fighter was hit into the ring of people, they would just shove him back into the action.

round — one section of a boxing match. Each round is three minutes long. There is a one-minute break between rounds.

saved by the bell — spared a knockout decision by the ringing of the bell at the end of a round. If a boxer is down and the bell rings to signal the end of the round before he is back up, he can continue to fight.

southpaw — a boxer who punches with his left hand.

split decision — a decision about a fight in which the judges do not unanimously agree on a winner.

tale of the tape — the list of a boxer's physical measurements. The tale of the tape lists such things as a fighter's age, height, weight, reach, chest size, and neck size.

technical knockout (TKO) — decision in a fight where a fighter gets back to his feet after being knocked down, but the referee doesn't think he can continue to fight without getting injured. The winning fighter is given credit for a technical knockout. The ref can also call a TKO if one boxer is getting badly beaten up or has **dropped his guard** (stops trying to defend himself.)

three-knockdown rule — rule that a boxer cannot be knocked down more than three times in a single round.

throw in the towel — to admit defeat in a boxing match. To show he no longer can or wants to fight, the boxer or his attendant throws his towel or sponge up into the air or into the center of the ring. Sometimes boxers actually do this, but these days the phrase is used figuratively.

unanimous decision — decision about a boxing match in which all judges choose the same boxer as winner.

Research Sources

The 1993 Information Please Sports Almanac. Mike Meserole, editor. New York: Houghton Mifflin, 1993.

The 1996 Information Please Almanac. Otto Johnson, editor. New York: Houghton Mifflin, 1996.

Ali, Muhammad, with Richard Durham. *The Greatest: My Own Story.* New York: Random House, 1975.

Deford, Frank. "The Best of Friends," *Sports Illustrated,* Volume 89, No. 2, 1998.

Lardner, Rex. *Ali: Again the Champion.* New York: Grosset and Dunlap, 1974.

Mack, William. "The Fight's Over, Joe," *Sports Illustrated,* Volume 85, No. 14, 1996.

Remnick, David. *King of the World: Muhammad Ali and the Rise of the American Hero.* New York: Random House, 1998.

Wallechinsky, David. *The Complete Book of the Olympics.* New York: Little, Brown, 1991.

www.courier-journal.com/ali

Young, Dick. "The Forty Who Changed Sports," *Sport Magazine,* Volume 77, No. 12, 1986.